Copyright © 2025 by Slant Leadership Group, LLC.

All rights reserved. This book or any portion thereof may not be reproduced or used in any manner whatsoever without the express written permission of the publisher except for the use of brief quotations in a book review.

Unless otherwise indicated, Scripture quotations are taken from the Holy Bible, English Standard Version. ESV® Text Edition: 2016. Copyright © 2001 by Crossway Bibles, a publishing ministry of Good News Publishers.

Printed in the United States of America

ISBN: 979-8-218-72607-2

www.JamesMWilson.com

DEDICATION

To all the leaders who carry a dream for something more.

For those who want to win at work and at home.

You are the reason this book exists.

CONTENTS

	Introduction	1
1	Clarifying Your Purpose	3
2	Calling vs. Purpose – Stop Confusing the Two	19
3	The Signal – Identifying the Tug on Your Heart	25
4	Listen and Learn	44
5	Aspire – Defining the Future You Want	58
6	Navigate – Creating a Path Forward	66
7	Transform – Becoming Who You're Called to Be	80
8	The Lies That Keep You Stuck	87
9	Don't Just Clarify—Commit	93
	Acknowledgments	98
	Endnotes	99

THE SLANT METHOD

A 5-STEP FRAMEWORK TO HELP LEADERS ALIGN SUCCESS WITH MEANING

INTRODUCTION

What if I told you that most people live their entire lives chasing a version of success that leaves them empty?

What if the answer you're looking for isn't more money, more influence, or even more time, but more clarity?

This isn't another motivational book filled with hype. It's a practical path to help you finally stop drifting and start living with conviction, purpose, and peace. You don't need another planner. You don't need another late-night strategy session. You need alignment between who God created you to be and what you do each day.

Over the last decade, I've helped leaders, entrepreneurs, and ministry-minded professionals find that alignment. And I've lived this process myself through failure, redemption, success, and faith-filled pivots. I created the SLANT Method because I was tired of watching high-achieving people quietly burn out, stuck in cycles of overachievement and spiritual confusion.

This book is for the leader who has "everything" but still feels like something's missing. It's for the believer who knows God has more for them but can't see the next step. It's for the father, the entrepreneur, the creative, the ministry leader, the woman with influence, or the man with vision but no direction.

By the time you finish this short but powerful book, you'll have a clear method to:

Understand the signal God is sending you,

THE SLANT METHOD

Reflect on the lessons that shaped you,

Dream without fear,

Build goals with systems that work,

And become the person your calling requires.

You're not as far off as you think.
Let's get clear. Let's go deep. Let's walk forward, together.

1 CLARIFYING YOUR PURPOSE

Let's talk about purpose. Say it with me, "purpose." Pause and let that word sit with you. Why? Because we're not just talking about purpose as a vague idea. We're diving into what it really means to live in purpose. Secondly, we'll look into how to clarify your calling.

Purpose is one of the most powerful concepts in life, yet for many high achievers, it remains one of the most elusive. Have you ever hit every financial milestone, only to wonder, "Is this all there is?" Maybe you've asked:

God, what am I really here for?

What's next for me?

What am I doing with my life?

Why do I still feel so unfulfilled?

If that's you, you're not alone. I've been there. Many of us wrestle with these questions, especially when success leaves us feeling empty rather than fulfilled. Clarifying your purpose is not about figuring out what you need to do next. It's about discovering who God has called you to be. When you focus on the "who," the "what" will follow.

When I Hit Rock Bottom

Let me take you back to 2007. I had just finished my first year in college. I was completely lost. I wasn't just failing my classes; I was failing at life. I ended my freshman year with a 1.0 GPA and earned academic probation. I hit rock bottom with no vision or clarity for my life. I dropped out and moved back in with my mom. Sad and embarrassed, I wrestled with questions like:

God, what am I supposed to do?

What's the point of all of this?

Where am I supposed to go from here?

I felt hopeless like I had nothing to offer anyone. Out of desperation, I started teaching drum lessons to kids. When that fizzled out, I took a job at a Christian daycare. On the surface, it wasn't glamorous. I spent my days picking up kids, helping them with homework, and playing games with them. At first, I treated it like just another job. But then, something shifted. I noticed how the kids responded to me:

"Mr. James, can we go outside to play?"

"Mr. James, thanks for being here."

"We love you, Mr. James!"

These weren't just cute moments; they were revelations.

God was showing me something I couldn't ignore: My value wasn't in what I was doing but in who He was calling me to be. He was shaping me into a leader. I was becoming someone others could trust, someone who builds relationships, and someone who makes an impact.

Your Purpose Starts with Who You Are

This was my turning point: I stopped obsessing over what job I needed, what career I'd build, what success should look like. Instead, I leaned into the "who" which changed everything.

The same is true for you. Clarifying your purpose starts with understanding your identity not in your achievements, your job title, or in other people's expectations. Stop chasing clarity in your circumstances and start seeking clarity in your identity. When you root yourself in who God has called you to be, you'll lead with purpose and live with impact at work, at home, and in the lives of those you serve.

Your identity is rooted in Christ Ephesians 2:19 reminds us: "So then you are no longer strangers and aliens, but you are fellow citizens with the saints and members of the household of God." Let that sink in. You are not an outsider in God's kingdom. You are not just another success story or someone fighting to hold it all together. You are a citizen of heaven, a member of God's family. That truth changes how you lead, how you love, and how you live.

False Identity Traps: The Lies High Achievers Believe

Before you can lead from your true identity, you have to recognize the false ones trying to run the show. Here are a few traps that high performers often fall into. Maybe you'll see yourself in one of them:

The Performer
"I am what I accomplish."
Your value rises and falls based on your output. Rest feels like failure, and you only feel worthy when you're producing.

The Provider
"I exist to take care of everyone else."
You're needed, dependable, and exhausted. But secretly, you wonder if you have permission to be more than everyone else's rock.

The Perfectionist
"If I'm not flawless, I'm a failure."
You carry silent pressure to get everything right. When you don't, you spiral in shame.

The Prover
"I have to earn love, respect, and success."
You hustle to prove you're not lazy, broken, or a fraud even if no one else is asking you to.

You're not what you do. You are who God says you are. Until you break free from these identity traps, true clarity will always feel just out of reach.

Living Out Your Identity

Understanding your identity in Christ isn't just a mental exercise. Here's how this plays out in key areas of your life:

In Your Family:
Your family sees the real you. Let your identity in Christ influence how you show up at home. Be the spouse, parent, or child God has called you to be. Lead with love, serve with humility, and reflect Christ's grace to those closest to you.

In Your Leadership:
Whether you're leading a business, a team, or your household, anchor your decisions in your identity. Leadership built on titles will crumble, but leadership built on Christ-centered identity will endure.

Are you leading with integrity, even when no one's watching?

Are you modeling faith, purpose, and clarity for those you serve?

Let me tell you a quick story about someone whose name you already know, but whose struggle may sound familiar. Howard Schultz, the former CEO of Starbucks, once stood on the stage of one of the most recognized companies in the world, overseeing billions in revenue, leading thousands of employees, and shaping global culture through coffee. At the height of his success, he confessed he felt deeply lost.

After stepping away from the company and then returning in 2008, he wrote in his memoir that despite all his accomplishments, he had disconnected from the very reason he started: to create a company that cared about people, not just profits. He said, "I had become so focused on scale and speed that I forgot what made us special."

Schultz realized he had allowed success to shape his identity. His decisions were rooted in performance, not purpose. He had to realigned himself with his original mission: treating employees with dignity, giving people a place of connection, and leading with his values. Once he did that, he regained clarity.

His journey reminds us of this truth: When identity is misaligned, even success can feel like failure. And if someone like Schultz, at the top of the business world, can feel lost, how much more do we need a foundation deeper than metrics, milestones, or money? That's why clarifying your purpose isn't about quitting your job or moving to another city. It's about coming back to the center. It's about asking, "Who has God called me to be, and how can I lead from that place?" When you root your identity in something eternal, not external, you lead differently. You live with clarity, not confusion. That's what we're after.

In Your Private Life:
The enemy often attacks when you're alone. The enemy whispers numerous lies about what you're not or will never become. But here's the truth: "My sheep listen to my voice; I know them, and they follow me" (John 10:27).

When you root yourself in Christ's identity, His voice rises above the noise. You don't need validation from the world. God's truth is the only voice that matters.

Hearing God's Voice Above the Noise

Picture this: You're in a crowded room full of noise, conversations, and distractions. But then your child calls out to you. Instantly, you recognize their voice. Why? Because you know them.

The same is true with God. In the chaos of life, busyness, responsibilities, and overwhelming noise, His voice remains constant. He knows you, and you can learn to recognize Him. But it starts with knowing who you are in Him.

When you are clear on your identity, the noise of the world fades. The pressure to measure up, perform, and prove your worth disappears. Instead, God's voice becomes unmistakable, guiding you toward clarity and purpose.

Remember This:
Your worth is not in what you accomplish; it's in what Christ has already done. When you embrace your identity in Him, every decision, every relationship, and every season of your life becomes clearer and more purposeful.

So ask yourself today:

Am I listening to God's voice or the world's noise?

Am I showing up as the person God has called me to be?

Let His voice shape your actions. Let His truth define your worth. Your identity is secure. Not in success, but in Christ.

Let Your Actions Follow Your Identity

Once you've rooted yourself in your identity in Christ, the next question is: "What do I do with this?" Purpose isn't just about knowing who you are; it's about allowing that knowledge to transform how you lead and live. Dr. Benjamin Hardy, a leadership expert, writes about envisioning the person you want to become and aligning your actions with that vision. For you, it's bigger than a vision. It's about becoming the leader God has called you to be.

You are not just a leader, manager, executive, business owner, or entrepreneur. At your core, you are a disciple of Christ. So, what does it look like to lead with both success and purpose? It's not about perfection. It's about showing up every day as the leader God has called you to be.

Here are three practical steps to ground your leadership in your identity:

1. **Stay Rooted in the Word** - Make Scripture a daily priority. Just as you review financial reports or strategy plans, start your day by aligning yourself with God's truth.

   Action Step: Spend 10 minutes each morning reading and reflecting on a passage that inspires your faith and leadership.

2. **Prioritize Prayer** - True leadership starts with communion with God. Prayer isn't about reciting fancy words; it's about staying connected to your ultimate source of wisdom.

   Action Step: Set aside time daily to talk to God about your business, your team, and your family. Invite Him to guide your decisions.

3. **Build Kingdom Relationships** - You don't have to carry the weight of leadership alone. Walk alongside others who share your faith and values. Encourage each other to live out your calling.

   Action Step: Schedule a weekly call or coffee meeting with another faith-driven leader. Join or create a mastermind group where you can grow spiritually and professionally.

The Power of Alignment

When you root your identity in Christ and let your actions follow, you begin leading from a place of clarity, confidence, and purpose. The noise of success, profit margins, accolades, or pressures begins to fade, and God's voice becomes unmistakable.

Your leadership is about more than success. It's about significance. Align your life and business with God's truth, and He will guide you to lead with greater purpose and impact than you ever imagined.

Ask yourself today:

Am I leading from my identity in Christ or from my achievements?

How can I take one step today to let God's truth shape my leadership?

Take that step. Show up. Trust God with the rest.

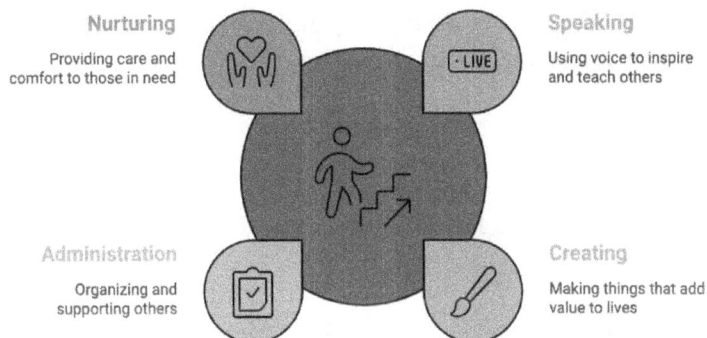

Integrating Purpose into Career Paths

Nurturing — Providing care and comfort to those in need

Speaking — Using voice to inspire and teach others

Administration — Organizing and supporting others

Creating — Making things that add value to lives

Bringing Purpose into Your Career

Your identity as a child of God shapes your purpose wherever you are including your career. Jesus said in Matthew 5:14–16: "You are the light of the world… let your light shine before others, that they may see your good deeds and glorify your Father in heaven." Your workplace is your mission field. Whether you lead a team, run a business, or work behind the scenes, God has placed you there to be a light. The question becomes: How can you use your God-given gifts to make an impact and serve others?

Here's What That Might Look Like:

If you're a communicator: Use your voice to inspire, teach, and encourage those around you. Speak with clarity and conviction that points others toward hope.

If you're a creator: Build, design, or innovate in ways that add value to people's lives and honor excellence.

If you're an organizer: Use your gift of administration to bring order, clarity, and support to teams and systems.

If you're a nurturer: Care for those who are struggling and be the steady presence they need.

The point isn't to fit yourself into someone else's definition of purpose. It's about recognizing the gifts God has entrusted to you and using them faithfully. You don't need to preach a sermon at work or wear your faith on your sleeve to make a difference. Instead, let your actions speak for you: Show up with excellence in your work. Lead with integrity when making decisions. Treat others with kindness and respect, even when it's difficult. Your work ethic, character, and service will reflect God's love.

Living Out Purpose in Family

As a leader, it's easy to pour your energy into your business or job while feeling disconnected at home. Maybe you're asking:

"What's my role in my family?"

"How can I build a family that honors God and feels connected?"

Let your actions follow your identity. If you're a child of God, then your purpose in your family is to reflect His love, grace, and faithfulness.

Practical Ways to Live with Purpose at Home:

As a spouse: Prioritize communication, connection, and sacrificial love. Be intentional about nurturing your marriage.

As a parent: Model faith and integrity for your children. Show them what it looks like to trust God, work hard, and love well.

As a sibling or child: Be quick to forgive, offer support, and build connections, even when it's inconvenient or difficult.

It's not about perfection or creating a flawless family dynamic. It's about showing up daily with love, humility, and intentionality. The small things like choosing patience over frustration, speaking life instead of criticism, or serving when no one's watching, are the building blocks of a purpose-driven family.

Leading With Purpose in Every Role

Your career and your family are not separate from your purpose; they're part of it. As a leader in the workplace and at home, let your identity in Christ shape how you show up. When you embrace your role as a faithful spouse, parent, leader, or entrepreneur, you'll find clarity and fulfillment in ways the world cannot offer.

Ask yourself today:

Am I bringing God's light into my workplace through my actions?

Am I living with intentionality in my family relationships?

Lead where you are, love where you are, and trust that God will multiply your impact. Your purpose starts with faithfulness in the season you're in right now.

The Power of Faithful Action

When you align your actions with your identity in Christ, you step into clarity, purpose, and impact. It's not about being perfect or having it all figured out. It's about taking the next faithful step by being obedient with what God has placed right in front of you and trusting Him with what's ahead. Your purpose isn't something you manufacture; it's something you discover as you faithfully live out your identity. Purpose doesn't start with a grand strategy or a perfect plan because it starts with faithfulness in the small things.

Living Out Your Identity in Every Area of Life

Once you are grounded in who you are in Christ, the next step becomes clear: Live it out. Align your actions with the truth of your identity. If you want to be a leader who reflects Christ, then act like the leader God has called you to be: Lead your family with love and integrity. Run your business with purpose and excellence. Show up for your team with humility and conviction.

If you want to be a loving, godly husband, leader, or parent, ask: What would a faithful follower of Christ do in this role? Take care of yourself physically, mentally, and spiritually. Keep your word. Integrity builds trust. Be present with your spouse and family. Lead with love, grace, and intentionality. Have the hard conversations but do so with humility and kindness.

When you don't know who you are in Christ, it's easy to chase roles or goals that don't align with God's calling. You'll find yourself saying "yes" to things that feel good in the moment but leave you overwhelmed, confused, and unfulfilled. But when you're rooted in your identity, your actions become purposeful, your priorities become clear, and your leadership has eternal impact. Matthew 6:33 says it best: "But seek first his kingdom and his righteousness, and all these things will be given to you as well." Focus on who you belong to, and God will align everything else.

If you're holding on to areas of your life that belong to God, you'll struggle with confusion and frustration. Speaking from experience, when I've tried to control what I was meant to surrender, it's never gone well. Maybe you silently believe, "God, you can have everything except my career, my habits, my money, and my family." God can't fully bless what you won't fully surrender.

When you let go and give God your all, clarity begins to replace confusion. Why? Because when Christ is Lord over everything, the steps you need to take flow naturally from your identity.

Clarity Comes from Alignment

When your actions align with your identity in Christ, purpose becomes clear. When you step outside of that alignment, when you compromise, hide sin, or chase the world's definition of success, chaos takes over.

For example:

If you're dishonest in business, it will create mistrust and confusion.

If you're neglecting your family while pursuing goals, you'll feel misaligned and empty.

If you're operating out of pride or control, it will trip you up and cloud your leadership.

God is not the author of confusion (1 Corinthians 14:33). He is the God of clarity and peace. He wants to guide you into a life of purpose, fulfillment, and impact. Alignment starts with surrender. Surrender your career decisions. Surrender your relationships. Surrender your vision for success. When you align every area of your life with God's truth, you'll step into the clarity and impact you were made for.

THE SLANT METHOD

A Daily Surrender

Living out your identity isn't a one-time decision, it's a daily surrender. As a high-achieving leader, I know this firsthand. The temptation to rely on our own wisdom, control every outcome, or measure success by worldly standards is strong. But every day, I've learned to pause and pray, asking God to help me live as the person He's called me to be.

When you let your actions flow from your identity, God will bring clarity. He will open doors, provide wisdom, and guide your next steps. When you know who you are, you'll begin to see what to do more clearly.

Reflect on These Questions:

What areas of my life do I need to surrender to God?

Are my actions aligned with my identity in Christ?

Am I truly trusting God, or am I still trying to control the outcomes on my own?

Clarity doesn't mean you'll have everything figured out today. It means trusting God one step at a time by focusing less on the future you're striving for and more on aligning your life with His purpose right now. High achievers like you often feel pulled in too many directions. You try to be everything for everyone, chasing bigger goals, and fighting distractions. But this kind of striving leads to burnout and confusion. This isn't about comparison or hustle. It's about letting go of control and filtering out distractions to focus on the mission God has given you. When you surrender, God will take care of what's ahead.

A Prayer for Clarity

Take a moment right now to pause and pray this with me:

"Father, I thank You for the life and gifts You've given me. Life moves so quickly, and the demands of leadership often pull me in every direction. But today, I choose to slow down and center my heart on You. I surrender every part of my life to You. My resources, my business, my family, and my future is yours. Remind me that I am first and foremost a citizen of heaven and Your child.

Lord, give me Your guidance. Provide me with peace and clarity. Open the doors You want me to walk through and close the ones that need to shut. Help me trust Your voice above the noise, walk in obedience, and lead with faith. In Jesus' name we pray, Amen."

Clarity doesn't come all at once. It comes through a daily rhythm of faith, trust, and surrender. As you take one step at a time, God will lead you into greater purpose and fulfillment. When your actions align with your identity in Christ, clarity replaces confusion, peace replaces overwhelm, and God's purpose becomes the guide for every area of your life. Take a deep breath, surrender, and trust Him with the journey ahead. He will show you the way.

CHAPTER 2: CALLING VS. PURPOSE – STOP CONFUSING THE TWO

Let's clear something up right now because if we don't, you'll spend the rest of this book chasing clarity with the wrong target in mind. Most people use the words calling and purpose interchangeably. But they are not the same.

Maybe you've said something like:

"I'm trying to figure out my calling."

"I just want to know my purpose."

"I'm successful, but I still don't feel aligned."

That last word "aligned" is where the tension lives. You're sensing that something is off. You've built a life, a business, a family, but it still doesn't feel quite… right. That's because when you confuse purpose with calling, you'll try to build the right thing in the wrong season.

Purpose: Why You're Here

Your purpose is constant. It's the big picture: the reason you exist. It is why God created you in the first place. Purpose is not seasonal. It's not circumstantial. It's eternal. You were created to glorify God, to love people, and to reflect His character in every area of life. That's your unchanging why.

Paul puts it this way in Ephesians 2:10: "For we are His workmanship, created in Christ Jesus for good works, which God prepared beforehand, that we should walk in them." (ESV) You were created with purpose in mind. Not to impress people. Not to accumulate titles. But to walk in the good works God prepared for you. When we talk about purpose, we're not asking, "What do I do for a living?" We're asking, "Why do I exist?"

Calling: What You're Assigned to Do Right Now

Your calling is how you live out your purpose in a specific season. It's a divine assignment that aligns with your purpose, but it can change over time. Think of it like this: Purpose is the umbrella. Calling is the assignment underneath it. Calling is specific. It's time-bound. It's personal. And if you hold too tightly to an old calling, you'll miss the new one God is trying to hand you.

Let me give you an example.

A Calling That Changed But Not the Purpose

In the Old Testament, Joseph had one overarching purpose: to preserve life. That purpose didn't change. But his callings certainly did.

First, he was a dreamer who received visions from God.

Then, his brothers sold him as a slave. He was later falsely accused and became a prisoner. However, God's plan for Joseph was greater than he could ever imagine. Joseph later became second in command over Egypt. Different roles. Different seasons. Same purpose. If Joseph had gotten stuck thinking his purpose was to stay in Canaan, he would've missed his calling in Egypt. If he had assumed prison was the final stop, he would've never stepped into palace leadership.

This is where so many leaders get stuck. They think: "This job is my calling." But what if God's shifting your calling to realign you with your purpose? What if your next season is waiting, but you're too attached to the last one to step into it?

Primary vs. Secondary Calling

This is why we need to make another distinction. I learned this from Dr. Dharius Daniels who is a pastor, coach, and entrepreneur.

There are two kinds of calling:

1. Primary Calling:

This is the same for every follower of Jesus. To glorify God, to love others, and to reflect His image in the world.

2. Secondary Callings:

These are the specific assignments God gives us to carry out our primary calling. This includes being a parent, a coach, a teacher, a pastor, an entrepreneur, a mentor, or a creative. These can, and often will, change over time. Your purpose never changes. Your callings will. Don't confuse the assignment with the identity.

Biblical Proof: Jesus and Paul

Jesus' purpose was to bring salvation and glorify the Father. But even He had different roles. He was a carpenter, a teacher, a healer, and ultimately, the Lamb of God.

Paul? Same story. His purpose was to glorify God and spread the gospel. But he was a tentmaker, a church planter, a missionary, and a writer. His calling evolved, but his purpose stayed the same.

In Acts 13:36, Scripture says: "For David, after he had served the purpose of God in his own generation, fell asleep…" David's purpose was to serve God. His calling took many forms: shepherd, warrior, king, worshiper. Don't get caught chasing a title when God is giving you a new task.

Why This Matters So Much

When you confuse purpose and calling, three things happen: You stay stuck in a past season. You think, "But I was so good at that!" Yes, but is God still in it? You chase clarity in the wrong direction. You ask, "What's my next job?" instead of, "Who am I called to become in this season?" You feel like a failure when a calling shifts. But you didn't fail. The season just changed. And God's not done with you.

A Practical Example

I've gone from failing out of college to teaching drum lessons… to working at a daycare… to full-time ministry… to leadership consulting… to authoring this book. At every turn, the calling shifted. But the purpose? That stayed the same: to help people live with clarity, identity, and alignment with who God created them to be.

What about you?

You may be called to lead your family right now. Or to start that business. Or to leave something behind. The question is not just "What's my purpose?" It's also, "What's my assignment right now?"

Clarify the Season You're In

Don't get so focused on what you're called to do that you forget who you're called to be. And don't let your last assignment define your next one. There is a delicate balance between purpose and calling.

Maybe you're not confused, you're just in transition. Maybe God is moving you into a new calling, and you're holding on to the old one out of fear or familiarity. Friend, that's not failure. That's growth. You need to know how to distinguish your purpose versus your calling. You need a filter.

Let This Be Your Filter

If you're wondering whether something is your purpose or your calling, use this simple filter:

<u>Does not change over time</u>
Purpose: Why you exist

<u>Can change over time</u>
Calling: What God is inviting you to do in this season
Assignment: The role or job through which you carry out the calling
Passion: What energizes or excites you
Profession: What you're paid to do (may or may not align with calling)

Let that clarity guide your next step.

Surrender to What's Next

What if the reason you're frustrated isn't because you've missed your purpose. but because you've outgrown your current assignment? What if you've heard the signal, but you've hesitated to respond because it doesn't look like what you expected. Clarity often comes when we stop clinging to the old and trust God with the new.

Before you chase another opportunity, slow down and ask:

"Is this a new calling?"

"Is God shifting me into a new assignment?"

"Does this align with my purpose or distract me from it?"

God doesn't waste seasons. But He also doesn't want you stuck in one He's called you out of. Let go of what was. Embrace what is. And step boldly into what's next.

CHAPTER 3: THE SIGNAL – IDENTIFYING THE TUG ON YOUR HEART

Can you feel it? That persistent tug deep within you, the quiet voice that refuses to be ignored. It's like a small pebble in your shoe that irritating you with every step. It's a lingering thought that keeps showing up no matter how hard you try to shake it. You know the feeling. It's the gnawing sense that, despite your success, something is missing.

You toss and turn at night thinking, "Is this all there is?" No matter how hard you try to suppress it, the feeling persists. I call this the Signal. The signal is more than a passing thought. It's a divine prompting from God that nudges you toward the greater purpose He has for your life. Some people call it a holy discontent or a divine agitation. Whatever you call it, the signal is a spark. It is an invitation to step into something bigger than yourself.

Most people struggle to understand the signal. They get overwhelmed trying to decode it, asking questions like, "What does this mean?" or "Where do I even start?" The signal is like a compass, pointing you in the right direction, even if the full map isn't clear yet.

Why The Signal Matters

The signal is God's way of stirring you up. He is waking you up to the calling He's placed on your life. But too many people ignore it, distracted by the noise of daily responsibilities, success, and comfort. But not you. The reason you're reading this book is because you've felt the signal. You know there's more for you. You feel the signal to more impact to make, more purpose to live, and more alignment to find.

That signal is telling you:
"You're not done yet. There's a reason you're here. There's a purpose for your gifts."

Why You Miss the Signal

If the signal is so important, why do so many people ignore it?

Here are four common reasons:

1. Noise
We fill every moment with motion: scrolling, striving, hustling. We've trained ourselves to be uncomfortable with stillness, so the signal gets drowned out by distraction.

2. Fear
We're afraid the signal will require change. What if God calls me away from something I worked hard to build? What if obedience costs me comfort, status, or certainty?

3. Doubt
We question whether it's really God or just a fleeting thought. So instead of praying through it, we push it aside and move on with business as usual.

4. Pride
Sometimes, we don't want to admit that the life we've built, successful as it seems, may not be fully aligned with our calling.

The signal won't scream, but it won't disappear either. The longer you ignore it, the more disruptive it becomes.

Ways People Experience the Signal

The signal doesn't always have a dramatic arrival. There are no flashing lights or booming voices. Often, it's subtle. It's a stirring in your soul, a thought that keeps resurfacing, or a story that refuses to leave you.

Here are six common ways people experience the signal:

1. **A Failure Overcome:** You've made a mistake or hit rock bottom in your past, and now you feel a deep desire to help others avoid the same struggle.

    Example: A leader who once failed financially now mentors entrepreneurs to build sustainable businesses without repeating the same mistakes.

2. **A Moral Wrong:** You've witnessed an injustice, and it stirs something in you that won't let go. You feel called to stand up, speak out, or take action.

    Example: A business owner advocates for ethical practices in their industry after witnessing widespread corruption.

3. **A Lesson Learned**: You've experienced life-changing

growth, and you can't help but share what you've learned to guide others.

Example: A father who overcame years of work-life imbalance now helps high-achieving leaders prioritize family while succeeding professionally.

4. **A Passion Sparked**: You've discovered something that lights you up. Or it's something you love doing and you feel called to teach, lead, or share it with others.

   Example: A gifted speaker feels energized every time they inspire an audience and decides to help others communicate their message with clarity.

5. **A Frustration Released**: You've hit your limit with a recurring problem. You're tired of tolerating it, and now you're determined to be the one who solves it.

   Example: An overwhelmed executive creates a process for leading teams without burnout and shares it with other leaders.

6. **A Problem Solved**: You've found a solution to something that held you back, and now you feel compelled to help others achieve the same breakthrough.

   Example: A leader who overcame years of self-doubt teaches others how to rediscover confidence and clarity in their calling.

John Mark Comer – The Pastor Who Couldn't Keep Going

John Mark Comer had it all by most ministry standards. He was the lead pastor of a fast-growing megachurch in Portland, Oregon. Thousands attended each week. Books were being published. Invitations rolled in. On the outside, it looked like he was living his calling. But on the inside, his soul was unraveling. He describes waking up anxious, rushing through meetings, and numbing out at night. Until one day, his mentor asked him a piercing question: "John Mark, who are you becoming?"

That question struck a nerve. He realized he was achieving more than ever, but becoming less like Jesus in the process. The pace of his life was unsustainable. The pressure was slowly crushing his joy, relationships, and soul.

The signal had been there for years: chronic exhaustion, disconnection from God, a longing for a slower, more intentional way of living. He'd just been too busy to notice or too afraid to confront it.

He made a radical shift. He stepped down from leading the megachurch. He simplified his life. And he began writing and teaching about the very thing God had been whispering to him all along: slow down. Return to rhythm. Rediscover your soul.

His story reminds us:

Success without alignment will eventually feel like failure.

When the signal speaks, listen. Your soul is trying to get your attention and so is God.

The Signal Is Your Invitation

The signal is not a burden. It's an invitation. God is showing you the next step toward the purpose He's created for you. Your responsibility is to listen and respond.

So ask yourself:

What is God stirring in my heart?

What problem, passion, or frustration keeps coming to mind?

How can I begin to act on what I'm feeling?

The signal may feel unclear at first, but trust this: God doesn't waste the longing He's placed inside of you. It's the starting point of something meaningful. Pay attention to the signal. It's leading you toward your calling. You don't have to figure it all out today. The signal doesn't require you to know the whole journey. All you need to do is take next faithful step.

Clarifying the Signal Framework

The signal you feel—the tug on your heart—isn't just a momentary thought; it's a divine invitation. But recognizing and responding to that signal requires intentional steps. Here's a practical framework to help you turn that spark into meaningful action:

1. The First Step: Recognizing the Signal

Every transformation begins with awareness. Signals often emerge from moments of discomfort, failure, or a deep sense of misalignment in life.

Honesty: Admit where you are and identify the areas of your life that feel misaligned.

Curiosity: Explore why this feeling exists without rushing to solve it.

Practical Step: Reflect on moments when you've felt stuck, unfulfilled, or unsettled. Ask:

What recurring frustrations or thoughts keep showing up?

When have I felt most alive or most restless?

Action Tip: Journal your reflections. Writing down patterns or key experiences can help you recognize the signals God is using to get your attention.

2. The Turning Point: Taking Action on the Signal

Clarity doesn't come from standing still. The turning point happens when you take intentional action, even if you don't have all the answers. For me, this meant returning home, enrolling in community college, and starting small. I began teaching drum lessons. The key here is to move forward in faith. The first action doesn't need to be perfect or monumental. It just needs to create momentum.

Practical Step:

Look at your current resources, relationships, and opportunities.

Identify one small step you can take today to act on the signal.

Examples:

Reach out to a mentor or someone you admire for advice.

Sign up for a class, workshop, or conference that aligns with your tug.

Volunteer or test out a small project that aligns with the signal.

Remember: Action opens doors. The more you move forward, the clearer your path becomes.

3. The Process: Deepening Commitment and Growth

For me, this phase involved balancing work, education, and ministry training. It required commitment, consistency, and resilience to build the foundation for my calling.

This step is about:

Refinement: Growing through challenges and setbacks.

Discipline: Developing habits and routines that support your growth.

Community: Surrounding yourself with people who encourage you and hold you accountable.

Practical Step:
Ask yourself:

What habits or disciplines do I need to adopt to grow in this direction?

What relationships or mentors can help me stay on course?

Action Tip: Lean into learning through books, mentorship, or practical experiences. Every setback is an opportunity for growth.

4. Reflection: Understanding the Purpose of the Signal

At some point, you need to step back and reflect on how far you've come. Reflection transforms your experiences into lessons and reveals how God has been using the signal to prepare you for a greater purpose. For me, looking back on my failures and growth revealed how every moment was preparing me for ministry. Your story is no different.

Practical Step: Take intentional time to reflect through journaling, prayer, or conversations with trusted mentors. Ask:

How has this signal shaped me?

What strengths have I developed through this process?

How can I use what I've learned to serve others?

Action Tip: Write down the lessons you've learned and celebrate your progress. Gratitude for the journey, even the challenges, will fuel your next steps.

Conclusion

Clarifying the signal is a transformative process that requires honesty, action, perseverance, and reflection. Each step builds on the other: Recognize the signal. Take intentional action to create momentum. Commit to growth through discipline and resilience. Reflect to understand the purpose behind the process.

This framework is a cycle. As you grow and evolve, new signals will arise. By following this path, you'll learn to trust the process and move forward in faith, knowing God is guiding you toward your calling.

You don't need the entire map to take the next step. Trust the signal, trust the process, and trust the One who gave you the signal in the first place. Clarity comes through action.

My Story of the Signal

I never envisioned becoming a pastor, God's grace, forgiveness, and mercy guided me along the way. From the failures of my early college days to the fulfillment of serving in ministry, this story reflects a path of redemption and purpose. As I currently serve as an Executive Pastor of Ministries in the Atlanta Metropolitan area, I look back at these pivotal moments to recognize God's hand in my life and to inspire others to pursue their calling.

1. The Signal: Academic Struggles at Belmont Abbey College

I graduated from high school in 2007 and enrolled at Belmont Abbey College. Despite receiving a scholarship to this Catholic institution, I struggled with discipline and motivation. My first semester was humbling, as I barely passed any classes. Over Christmas break, regret set in, and I promised myself I would improve in the spring. Yet, I ended the year on academic probation.

Lacking a solid foundation of values, I made unethical decisions, and my GPA was embarrassingly low. Unable to face returning, I dropped out and moved back home with my mother in Charlotte, NC. This period was marked by failure, but it was the first of many signals that I needed a change.

2. The First Step: Finding Stability at Community College

Returning home, I began taking classes at Central Piedmont Community College (CPCC) while volunteering at my church in Pineville, SC. Teaching drum lessons at a local music store became my side hustle. Initially, I found teaching challenging, but by incorporating games into my lessons, I engaged the children and began enjoying my work.

Though I was making progress, the music store's policies left me feeling exploited. I eventually quit, leaving me without a job and questioning my next steps. Still, these experiences planted seeds that would later bear fruit.

3. The Turning Point: Activities Director at GraceLife Academy

Desperate for a flexible job, I reached out to my youth pastor, Stephen. He offered me a position at GraceLife Academy, a daycare affiliated with our church. Despite my initial hesitation, I accepted and began working as an after-school teacher for elementary-aged children.

This role became a turning point. As I built relationships with the kids, played games, and taught them Bible lessons, I recognized a gift for teaching about Jesus. Seeing the children's excitement inspired me, and I felt a growing call to ministry. Pastor Stephen's mentorship played a significant role, as he modeled ethical leadership and encouraged me to pursue my calling.

---

4. The Process: Pastor-in-Training (PIT) Program

With Pastor Stephen's guidance, I explored the idea of ministry more seriously. He connected me with our church's leadership team, and I eventually enrolled in the Pastor-in-Training (PIT) program. This two-year journey involved early-morning Bible studies, leading Awana programs, and serving in Children's Ministry. During this time, I balanced my responsibilities at CPCC, GraceLife Academy, and the PIT program.

Books on ministry became my passion, and prayer deepened my relationship with God. My calling became undeniable, and with my wife Alison's support, I prepared for full-time ministry. Though rejection letters initially discouraged me, persistence paid off when I accepted a Children's Coordinator position at a church in Hattiesburg, MS, in 2014.

5. Reflection: God's Grace in My Journey

Looking back, I see how God used each failure and success to prepare me for ministry. From academic probation to ethical dilemmas at the music store, each challenge taught me valuable lessons. Ethical leadership became a cornerstone of my ministry, as I learned to admit mistakes, seek forgiveness, and lead with integrity.

In 2022, I earned my bachelor's in religious studies, a

milestone that reaffirmed God's faithfulness. In 2023, I earned me master's in organizational leadership. Now, I serve as an Executive Pastor of ministries in a local church while being the founder and owner of Slant Leadership Group, LLC. My story is one of hope and redemption, reminding me that God never gives up on us. As a pastor, author, coach, and consultant, I am committed to helping others find their purpose and follow Jesus.

Biblical Examples of the Signal

If you're unsure whether you've experienced the signal, let's look at a few people in the Bible who felt it. These individuals didn't hear an audible voice from God but felt a clear tug that sparked them into action:

Nehemiah
Signal: Nehemiah felt a deep burden for the broken walls of Jerusalem when he heard about the city's state.
Key Verse: "As soon as I heard these words I sat down and wept and mourned for days, and I continued fasting and praying before the God of heaven." (Nehemiah 1:4, ESV)

Esther
Signal: Esther recognized her role in saving the Jewish people through Mordecai's challenge.
Key Verse: "And who knows whether you have not come to the kingdom for such a time as this?" (Esther 4:14, ESV)

Ruth
Signal: Ruth's loyalty to Naomi and her commitment to follow Naomi's God reflected her calling.

Key Verse: "Where you go I will go, and where you lodge I will lodge. Your people shall be my people, and your God my God." (Ruth 1:16, ESV)

Gideon
Signal: Gideon questioned Israel's oppression, showing his burden before being explicitly called.
Key Verse: "And Gideon said to him, 'Please, my lord, if the Lord is with us, why then has all this happened to us?'" (Judges 6:13, ESV)

Barnabas
Signal: Barnabas sold his property to support the early church, demonstrating his generosity and calling.
Key Verse: "Joseph, who was also called by the apostles Barnabas (which means son of encouragement), sold a field and brought the money to the apostles' feet." (Acts 4:36-37, ESV)

The Signal Quadrant: Understanding Your Reaction to Signals

The Signal Quadrant is a powerful framework for evaluating how you respond to life's signals—those tugs, nudges, or moments of discomfort that demand your attention. By plotting feelings (your emotional connection to a signal) on the X-axis and urgency (the perceived need to act) on the Y-axis, the quadrant reveals four possible responses: Avoidance, Awareness, Obligation, and Embrace.

Each quadrant tells a story about how you approach

opportunities, challenges, or growth. Let's break it down:

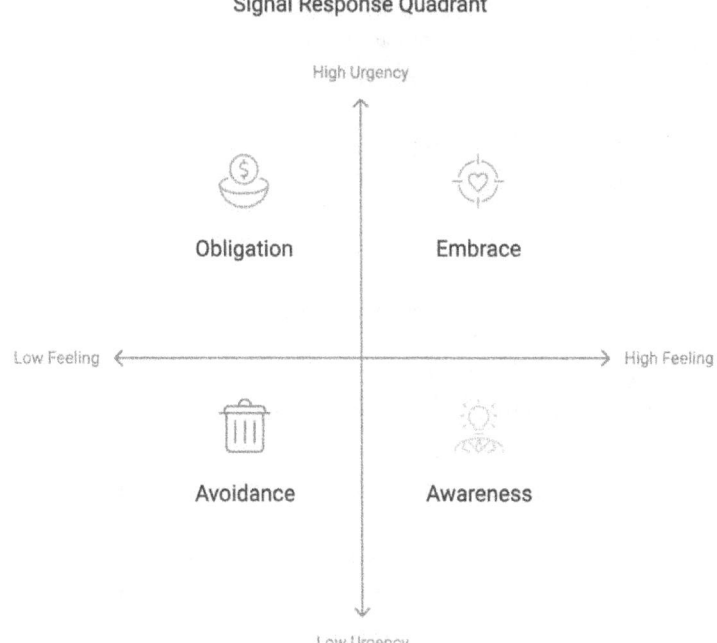

1. Avoidance (Low Feeling, Low Urgency)

When both feelings and urgency are low, the default response is Avoidance. In this state, a signal doesn't resonate emotionally, and there's no perceived pressure to act. It's easy to dismiss or ignore it.

Example: You notice a small issue in your business. Maybe you are dealing with a process inefficiency, but it feels insignificant, and there's no immediate need to address it. You avoid it altogether.

Result: While avoidance feels harmless initially, neglected signals in this quadrant can snowball into much larger problems if left unaddressed.

Question to Ask: Is there something I'm ignoring that could become a bigger issue later?

2. Awareness (High Feeling, Low Urgency)

When you feel a strong emotional connection to a signal but there's no immediate urgency, you land in the Awareness quadrant. This is a place of reflection and acknowledgment. You know it matters, but you're postponing action.

Example: You feel a pull to prioritize your health or spend more time with family. You acknowledge the importance but tell yourself, "I'll get to it soon."

Result: Awareness is a powerful starting point, but without urgency, action can remain a distant idea.

Question to Ask: What small step can I take to nurture this signal and create momentum?

3. Obligation (Low Feeling, High Urgency)

When urgency is high but emotional connection is low, you

respond out of Obligation. In this state, you take action because you feel you have to, not because you're personally invested.

Example: A client demands a last-minute project, and while you don't care deeply about it, you scramble to get it done because of external pressure.

Result: Obligatory action produces results but often drains you. It lacks purpose, fulfillment, and alignment with your values.

Question to Ask: Is this task necessary, or am I acting out of obligation at the cost of my greater purpose?

4. Embrace (High Feeling, High Urgency)

This is where transformation happens. When both feelings and urgency are high, you enter the Embrace quadrant. Here, the signal resonates deeply with you, and you recognize the need to act immediately. This is where growth, clarity, and alignment occur.

Example: You feel a deep calling to repair a broken relationship or pursue a passion project that aligns with your purpose. You sense that waiting will only cause regret, so you act decisively.

Result: Embracing signals leads to meaningful progress, alignment with your identity, and a greater sense of fulfillment.

Question to Ask: What signal am I ready to embrace right now, and what's the first step I can take?

Using the Quadrant in Your Life

The Signal Quadrant isn't just a framework. It's a mirror to evaluate where you are and where you need to shift. Use it to assess your current signals and your responses.

Reflection Questions:

Are there signals I'm avoiding that need my attention?

What signals am I aware of but failing to act on?

Am I caught in obligation, doing things without passion or purpose?

What signals am I ready to embrace, and how can I act on them today?

Your Goal: Moving to Embrace

The most meaningful progress happens in the Embrace quadrant. This occurs when you act on what feels deeply important and immediately necessary. This is where you align your life and leadership with God's purpose for you.

Identify one signal in your life right now. Where does it fall in the quadrant? If it's in Avoidance, Awareness, or Obligation, what will it take to move it toward Embrace?

Acting on your signals doesn't require perfection. Instead, it requires courage, clarity, and a willingness to take the next step. Lean into the signals God is showing you, and trust that He's guiding you toward something greater.

If this chapter stirred something in you, if you're waking up to the fact that your life or leadership is out of alignment, know this: you don't have to figure it all out alone.

I work with high-capacity leaders, entrepreneurs, and teams who are ready to stop drifting and start building with clarity. If you'd like help discerning your next step, visit www.JamesMWilson.com. You'll find options for personal coaching, team alignment intensives, and strategy sessions to help you move forward with confidence.

CHAPTER 4: LISTEN AND LEARN

In the SLANT framework, "Listen and Learn" is the step where we evaluate past experiences, reflect on patterns, and draw lessons to guide our path forward. I remember one evening after a particularly challenging day in ministry, I sat down to reflect on how I arrived at that moment. As I considered the day's events, I began to see how each challenge was tied to past decisions and experiences. It became clear that listening to and learning from these moments wasn't just helpful—it was essential for discerning God's direction and purpose in my life. The mistakes, the small victories, and even the moments I wanted to quit all painted a clear picture of God's hand in my life. This reflection reminded me that listening to our journey isn't just about acknowledging what happened—it's about discerning God's voice in the process. Each step, even the missteps, plays a role in shaping our calling.

This chapter focuses on how listening to your own story, learning from key moments, and discerning God's voice can provide clarity and direction. Listening and learning are not passive actions; they require intentionality and humility. By evaluating what has shaped you, you can identify opportunities for growth and steps toward your calling.

Listening to the Signals of Your Past

Your past holds countless signals that point toward your calling. These signals often come in the form of successes, failures, and pivotal experiences. Listening to your past doesn't mean dwelling on mistakes but learning from them. For example, when Peter in the Bible faced moments of doubt and denial, those experiences later became lessons that reshaped his faith and purpose. Similarly, your own story carries moments that have shaped who you are today.

Reflecting on your past is not always easy. It can feel uncomfortable to revisit failures or missed opportunities, but those moments often hold the clearest lessons. Take a moment to pause and reflect: What are the key moments in your life that have shaped your sense of purpose? Think about significant successes, failures, or turning points. For example, was there a moment when you felt God's presence guiding you through a challenge, or a time when a failure taught you a lesson you've carried forward? Write these moments down and consider how they reveal patterns or signals pointing to your calling. Write them down, and consider how they connect to where you are today.

These reflections can serve as a foundation for understanding God's direction in your life. As you look back, patterns often emerge like repeated opportunities to help others, moments of clarity during prayer, or specific skills and passions God has cultivated in you over time. These patterns and themes are not random; they are often God's way of pointing you toward your unique calling. Take time to identify these recurring threads, as they can illuminate the purpose God has prepared for you. As you reflect, consider asking yourself: "What signals in my past point to God's calling in my life?" "How have my successes and failures shaped my understanding of my purpose?" and "What patterns or themes keep reappearing in my journey that I should pay attention to?"

For example, I remember struggling with procrastination during a key project in my early career. This failure taught me the importance of discipline and prioritization, lessons that I later applied in ministry leadership. By addressing procrastination, I was able to meet deadlines and guide my team more effectively, reinforcing the significance of learning from past mistakes. The project didn't meet expectations, and I felt defeated. However, when I revisited that failure, I realized that my lack of organization and communication contributed to the outcome. That insight helped me develop better systems and habits, which have been instrumental in my growth ever since.

These guideposts from our past can show us what worked, what didn't, and where we might go next. They are like guideposts, showing you what worked, what didn't, and where you might go next. As you reflect, ask yourself, "What is God revealing through these experiences?" Listening to these signals takes courage, but that courage is necessary to move forward with purpose and clarity.

Sarah Blakely – Learning from Failure on Purpose

Before Sarah Blakely became the billionaire founder of Spanx, she sold fax machines door to door. She faced rejection constantly. Day after day, doors slammed, people laughed, and nobody took her seriously.

But here's the twist: Sarah didn't see it as failure because her dad had redefined the word for her.

Growing up, he asked her and her brother the same question at dinner every week:

"What did you fail at this week?"

If they didn't have an answer, he was disappointed.

That one question changed her life. It taught her that failure wasn't something to fear. It was proof you were trying, learning, and growing. She began to see each setback as a stepping stone, not a stop sign.

Later, when she came up with the idea for footless pantyhose and had no fashion or business experience, she heard every kind of "no" you could imagine. But she kept going. She listened to the lessons rejection was teaching her, instead of running from them.

Sarah didn't have a business degree, a wealthy network, or industry connections. What she did have was a pattern of learning from the past and turning pain into progress.

Her story reminds us: Failure isn't the opposite of success, it's the foundation of it. Your past struggles may feel like roadblocks. But if you stop and listen, you'll find they've actually been preparing you all along.

Why We Avoid Reflecting on Our Past

For many high-achievers, reflection sounds good in theory but terrifying in practice. Why? Because looking back means facing parts of your story you'd rather forget. Here are a few common reasons we avoid it:

Shame
"If I go back, I'll fall apart."
We're afraid that revisiting our past will reopen wounds we've buried under success and busyness.

Perfectionism
"I should be past this by now."
You hold yourself to impossible standards and believe reflection equals regression. But growth doesn't mean forgetting. It means learning.

Hustle Mindset
"Who has time to look back when I'm trying to move forward?"
We confuse movement with progress and forget that momentum without direction leads to burnout.

God doesn't waste your past. He recycles every piece of it into your purpose.

Breaking Old Habits

Sometimes, the process of listening and learning reveals old habits that no longer serve your purpose. Breaking these habits is essential for growth. They act as roadblocks, preventing us from stepping fully into God's plan for our lives. Peter's story is a powerful example of how breaking old habits leads to personal transformation and the fulfillment of purpose. His struggles with fear and denial mirror the challenges many of us face today whether it's battling insecurity, unhealthy patterns, or a reluctance to step into God's calling.

These modern-day struggles remind us that, like Peter, we must confront and let go of what holds us back in order to fully embrace the transformative work of the Holy Spirit in our lives. Before his transformation, Peter struggled with fear, lies, and selfishness. When questioned about his relationship with Jesus, he denied Him three times out of fear for his own safety. But after being filled with the Holy Spirit, Peter became bold and unwavering in his faith, proclaiming the gospel even in the face of persecution.

We all have old habits that hold us back. They may not always be as visible as Peter's denials, but they can be just as limiting. Maybe it's fear, procrastination, or unhealthy patterns. These habits keep us tethered to the past, preventing us from stepping into God's greater plan. Letting go of them requires boldness and trust in God. It's not just about changing behavior; it's about allowing the Holy Spirit to bring about internal transformation.

The beauty of Peter's story is that God didn't give up on him, even when he stumbled. Instead, He used those failures as a foundation for growth. This reminds us that our own shortcomings do not disqualify us from God's purpose. In fact, they often prepare us for it. The process of breaking old habits can feel overwhelming, but it starts with trusting God to work through you.

Learning from Others

Listening and learning are not solitary practices. Much of what we learn comes through relationships with others. In my own journey, mentors have been invaluable in helping me discern my calling. Biblical examples also illustrate how listening to signals and learning from others can clarify one's purpose. Consider Moses, who was hesitant to lead the Israelites out of Egypt. Through God's guidance and the mentorship of his brother Aaron, Moses learned to trust God's call despite his initial fears and doubts. Similarly, Paul's transformation on the road to Damascus was followed by mentorship from Ananias, who helped Paul understand his new purpose as a messenger of Christ.

These stories show us that listening to God's signals and learning from those He places in our lives are crucial steps toward embracing our calling. These relationships remind us that growth often happens in community, not in isolation. Mentors, friends, and even adversaries can provide insights that shape our path. In Peter's case, Jesus Himself was the ultimate mentor, guiding and challenging Peter to grow in his faith.

Think about the people in your life who have influenced you. Some may have encouraged you, while others may have challenged you in ways that forced you to grow. Both are valuable. Wisdom often comes from unexpected places, and being open to learning from others enriches your journey. Even moments of conflict can teach you patience, humility, and how to rely on God.

The Holy Spirit also acts as a guide, convicting and directing us toward God's will. This is not something we can achieve alone. We need the influence of others and the guidance of the Spirit to fully grasp what God is teaching us.

Peace as a Byproduct of Faith

As you learn to listen to God and reflect on the signals in your life, you begin to experience peace, not a worldly peace that comes and goes, but a deep, lasting peace that only God can provide. Romans 12:18 reminds us, "If possible, so far as it depends on you, live peaceably with all." Peace starts with receiving it from God. When you spend time in His Word and in prayer, you align your heart with His, allowing Him to calm your fears and anxieties.

This peace also extends to others. While you can't control how others respond to you, you can choose to live in a way that reflects Christ's love. As Paul says, "So far as it depends on you." The effort to live peaceably is an act of faith and obedience, even when it's difficult.

Transformation Through Boldness

The lessons we learn are meant to lead to action. Transformation happens when we take what we've learned and use it to align our lives more closely with God's purpose. Peter's story shows this vividly. After denying Jesus out of fear, he later stood before the same people who crucified Jesus and boldly proclaimed His name. That kind of transformation is only possible through faith and the power of the Holy Spirit.

Boldness doesn't mean the absence of fear; it means choosing to act in faith despite it. I remember a time when my wife and I felt God calling us to take a significant step of faith by transitioning into full-time ministry. That decision required us to leave behind the comfort of predictability and face the unknown with bold trust in God. It wasn't easy, financial uncertainty and doubt loomed large, but we chose to act in faith. That leap not only deepened our reliance on God but also transformed how we viewed His provision and guidance in our lives. We didn't have all the answers, and the financial uncertainty was daunting. But we trusted God's leading, and that bold decision ultimately opened doors we never imagined. This kind of boldness is about stepping forward, even when the outcome isn't clear, because you trust that God is guiding the way.

When you listen to God's voice and learn from your experiences, you gain the clarity and courage needed to take those steps. The Holy Spirit equips us to break free from old habits and step into the purpose God has for us. You can't make disciples or fulfill your calling without breaking the habits that hold you back. Transformation requires both surrender and courage, and God provides both when we ask.

Conclusion

"Listen and Learn" is not just a step in a process; it is a way of life. By tuning into the signals of your past, seeking wisdom from others, and allowing the Holy Spirit to guide you, you can experience the kind of transformation that Peter did. Reflect on the signals God has placed in your life, identify the habits or patterns that need to change, and lean into the guidance of mentors and the Holy Spirit. These steps not only clarify your calling but also equip you to take bold actions in alignment with God's purpose for your life.

This journey requires humility and boldness, but the rewards are eternal. Your story, with all its highs and lows, is part of a greater narrative that God is writing. When you listen and learn, you become an active participant in that story, moving closer to the purpose for which you were created.

The Listening and Learning Framework

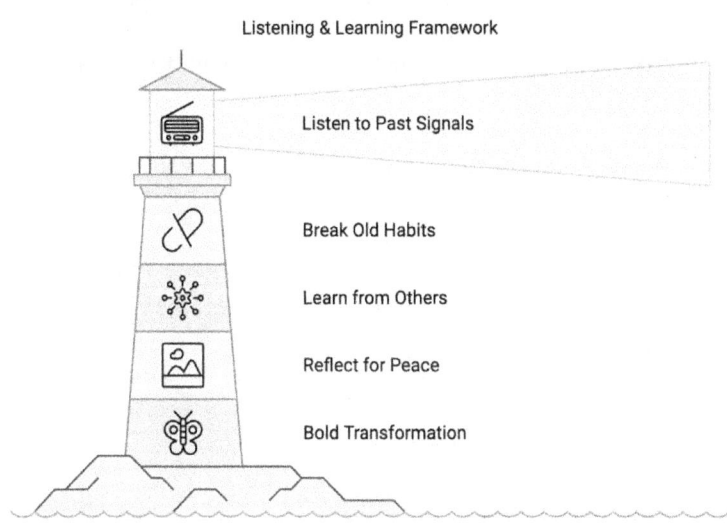

To guide you through this process, here is a framework that breaks "Listen and Learn" into actionable steps:

1. Listen to the Signals of Your Past

What It Means: Your past holds countless signals that point toward your calling. These signals often come in the form of successes, failures, and pivotal experiences. Listening to your past is not for dwelling on mistakes, but for learning.

Example: When Peter in the Bible faced moments of doubt and denial, those experiences later became lessons that reshaped his faith and purpose. Similarly, your own story carries moments that have shaped who you are today.

Action Steps:

Reflect on your successes, failures, and turning points.

Ask yourself: "What signals in my past point to God's calling in my life?"

Write down key moments and consider how they connect to where you are today.

Look for recurring themes or patterns, such as opportunities to lead, moments of compassion, or times when you felt God's guidance.

2. Break Old Habits

What It Means: Sometimes, the process of listening and learning reveals old habits that no longer serve your purpose. Breaking these habits is essential for growth and transformation.

Example: Peter struggled with fear, lies, and selfishness before his transformation. However, after being filled with the Holy Spirit, he became bold and unwavering in his faith, proclaiming the gospel even in the face of persecution.

Action Steps:

Identify habits or patterns that are holding you back, such as fear, procrastination, or unhealthy behaviors.

Pray for God's help in letting go of these habits.

Trust in the Holy Spirit to bring about internal transformation.

Take one bold step toward breaking a limiting habit, even if it feels uncomfortable.

3. Learn from Others

What It Means: Listening and learning are not solitary practices. Much of what we learn comes through relationships with others, whether mentors, friends, or even adversaries.

Example: Moses relied on the mentorship of Aaron to step into his calling, and Paul's transformation was guided by Ananias. Similarly, Jesus mentored Peter, guiding him through his doubts and preparing him for leadership.

Action Steps:

Reflect on the people in your life who have influenced you positively or challenged you to grow.

Seek guidance from mentors, pastors, or trusted friends who can help clarify your calling.

Be open to learning even in moments of conflict or difficulty.

Pray for wisdom and discernment in understanding what God is teaching you through others.

4. Pursue Peace Through Reflection

What It Means: As you learn to listen to God and reflect on the signals in your life, you begin to experience a peace that only God can provide. This peace is a byproduct of aligning with His purpose.

Example: Romans 12:18 says, "If possible, so far as it depends on you, live peaceably with all." By reflecting on God's guidance and trusting His plans, you can find peace even in uncertain times.

Action Steps:

Spend time in prayer and scripture to align your heart with God's.

Reflect on how peace might signal alignment with God's will.

Choose to act in ways that reflect Christ's love, even when others may not respond in kind.

Trust God's promises and allow Him to calm your anxieties.

5. Take Bold Steps Toward Transformation

What It Means: The lessons we learn are meant to lead to action. Transformation happens when we use what we've learned to align our lives more closely with God's purpose.

Example: After denying Jesus, Peter later stood boldly before the same people who crucified Him, proclaiming His name.

This transformation was possible through faith and the power of the Holy Spirit.

Action Steps:

Identify one area where God is calling you to step out in faith.

Take intentional, bold actions, trusting God to guide the outcome.

Reflect on how each step of boldness brings you closer to fulfilling your purpose.

Celebrate small victories as evidence of God's transformative work in your life.

CHAPTER 5: ASPIRE – DEFINING THE FUTURE YOU WANT

What Does It Mean to Aspire to Something Bigger?

"Where there is no vision, the people perish." – Proverbs 29:18

Aspiring to something bigger begins with a simple yet powerful act: dreaming. To aspire means to look beyond where you are, imagine what's possible, and believe that God has placed a greater purpose inside of you.

Too often, life pulls us in different directions, leaving us aimless and drifting. But drifting never leads to growth or success. It takes clarity and vision to build a meaningful future.

As the year draws to a close, many of us begin to reflect. We think about what we want to accomplish, who we want to become, and the impact we want to make. It's not enough to just think about it. You need to write it down, because goals give direction to your decisions.

For me, every year starts the same way: with dreaming. I sit down with a journal and begin to write. I dream about the life I want to live: the work I want to do, the impact I want to make, the vacations I want to take, the health I want to achieve, and the relationships I want to strengthen.

How to Set Meaningful Goals Aligned with Your Purpose

Dreaming is the starting point, but meaningful goals are the steps that turn dreams into reality. I want you to think about these areas of your life:

Faith (your relationship with God)

Family (marriage, parenting, and extended family)

Finances (financial goals, giving, and saving)

Fitness (physical and mental health)

Vocation (career and calling)

Avocation (hobbies, travel, and personal interests)

Write down one or two goals for each area. Don't focus on perfection, just focus on clarity. A vague goal like "I want to be a better husband" is still a starting point. It will help you make decisions that align with that vision.

And remember: the goals you make determine the actions you take.

The Aspire Framework: 5 Steps to Defining Your Future

Over the years, I've developed a simple framework to help me move from dreaming to doing. I call it the Aspire Framework:

Dream
Start by dreaming big. What does your ideal future look like? Who do you want to become? Ask God for clarity on what He wants to do through you.

Example: Dream about the health you want to achieve, the marriage you want to build, or the impact you want to make in your community.

Focus
Focus is about saying no to distractions and yes to what matters. Without focus, you'll drift aimlessly, saying yes to opportunities that don't align with your goals.

"I've never drifted to success. I've never drifted to a healthier marriage. I've never drifted to getting work done."
Write down your priorities and let them guide your daily choices.

Consistency
Consistency is where transformation happens. It's about building habits. The small choices you make daily add up over time.

Story: When I set a goal to ride a 30-mile bike race, I didn't get there overnight. I trained week by week, mile by mile, until I was ready. Consistency got me to the starting line.

Execute
Execution is about action. Do the work, but don't sacrifice

your health, family, or faith in the process. God calls us to be effective, not burned out.

Tip: Practice deep work. Turn off distractions, set a timer, and focus on your most important tasks.

Flexibility
Life doesn't always go as planned. Situations change, goals evolve, and God redirects our path. Be willing to adapt. If a goal isn't working, realign, adjust, or eliminate it.

Let me show you what it looks like when someone doesn't just dream big, but dreams with God, aligns their life, and makes decisions that honor Him at every level of success.

David Green – When God Redefines Success

David Green didn't set out to build a billion-dollar empire. He started small, assembling picture frames in his garage with a $600 loan. But over time, that humble beginning turned into Hobby Lobby, one of the largest arts and crafts retailers in the nation.

From the outside, it looked like the American Dream: success, wealth, legacy. But David Green wasn't chasing the world's version of success—he was chasing God's vision for his life.

As the company grew, he faced decisions that tested his values. He chose to close all Hobby Lobby stores on Sundays. This was a move that defied retail norms but aligned with his faith. He committed to giving away over half of the company's profits, funding Bibles, missions, and Christian education. And he publicly said that everything he owns belongs to God, not him. When asked about it, he said: "The more Hobby Lobby has grown, the more I've realized that I don't own anything. I'm just a steward of what God has entrusted to me."

David didn't just dream big; he dreamed with God. He aspired not for applause, but for obedience. Not for influence, but for impact. Here's what his life teaches us: Success isn't what you build it's what you surrender. When you let God define your future, you may still achieve great things. But the purpose behind your success will feel eternal, not empty.

Aspiration without alignment will wear you out. But aspiration rooted in God's purpose will bring peace, clarity, and kingdom-level impact.

Maybe by now, you're starting to feel inspired. But if there's a voice inside still whispering, "Dreaming is dangerous…"—you're not alone.

Why Dreaming Feels Dangerous

For many leaders, the idea of dreaming feels less like inspiration and more like risk.

Disappointment
"Last time I dreamed big, I got burned."
You stepped out before, only to feel like you failed. The pain of unmet expectations has made you cautious.

Comparison
"Other people's dreams look better than mine."
You scroll through highlight reels, wondering if your vision is too small, too slow, or too ordinary to matter.

Limiting Beliefs
"That's just not realistic for someone like me."
Whether it's your past, circumstances, or doubts, you've convinced yourself that dreaming big is for "other people."

Dreaming with God is not fantasy. It's faith in motion. When He gives the dream, He provides the strength to pursue it. The risk isn't dreaming too big. The real risk is playing it safe and missing what He placed in your heart on purpose.

What Does Your Life Look Like When You Succeed?

When you dream big, focus on what matters, stay consistent, execute well, and remain flexible, you'll start to see a vision unfold that's greater than you imagined.

For me, that vision has taken me from dropping out of college with a 1.0 GPA to finishing my master's degree with a 4.0. It's allowed me to pursue my passion for leadership, speak into people's lives, and help leaders clarify their calling.

Success isn't about perfection it's about progress. It's about trusting God's plan, staying faithful in the process, and becoming the person He created you to be.

Action Step

Take 20 minutes today to:

Dream about the future you want.

Write down one goal for each area of your life (faith, family, finances, fitness, vocation, avocation).

Commit to taking one small action toward each goal this week. Aspiration starts with clarity, but it's built with action. Let's get to work.

The Aspire Framework Pyramid

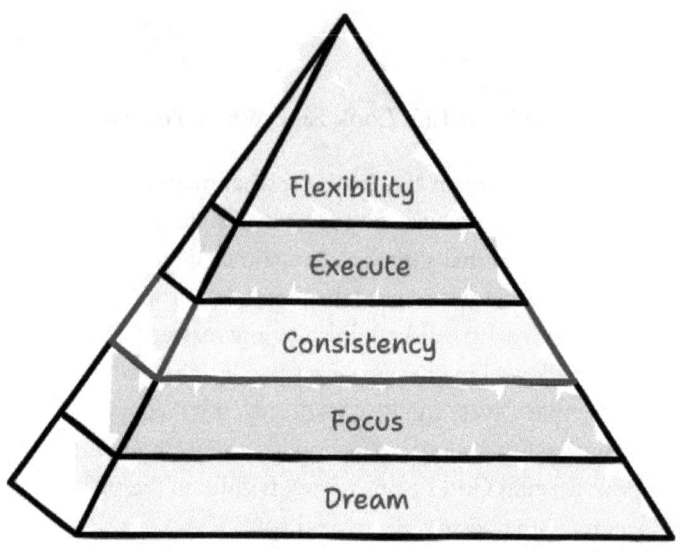

A Word of Caution on Dreaming

Remember when you were a kid? Your imagination ran wild, free from constraints. You'd jump off the couch, build forts, and make up games. As a child, you believed anything was possible. But as you grew older, you started hearing the word "no." That one little word is often a dream killer. As an adult, you've likely stopped dreaming. You aspire to more, but your mind begins to focus on logistics, reasons why it can't happen, and the resources required to achieve your goals. Stress rises, and before long, you quit your dream before you've even started.

THE SLANT METHOD

That is the old way. Leave it in the past. You will no longer throw your dreams away because of doubt or frustration. But how is this possible? If your dreams are important yet built on a shallow foundation, they will never survive. Dreaming is the foundation of the pyramid for a reason. Instead of focusing solely on your wants and needs, let me offer a perspective shift.

I believe God gives us dreams to pursue for Him. I trust that God will provide for me as I follow His lead. I use the gifts He has given me to serve others. I recognize that my time on earth is limited, which fuels my relentless focus. I also believe that if I don't use my gifts, God will find someone else who will. With this perspective, I dream confidently, knowing the dream does not belong to me. It is God's assignment for me. This shift replaces the focus off us and places God where He in the center.

When you focus solely on your wants and needs, the pressure intensifies. The weight of the future can feel crushing. However, when you understand that your dreams are God's assignments, you feel energized and at peace. God's assignments are not easy or trouble-free, but there is a deep joy in knowing His provision and protection will go with you as you pursue them.

As you dream, resist the urge to place your limitations on God's assignments. Receive and believe what He has for you. Dream first. Focus later.

CHAPTER 6: NAVIGATE – CREATING A PATH FORWARD

One of the most overwhelming parts of pursuing your calling is figuring out how to begin. The vision ahead might seem exciting, but the path forward can feel daunting. You may find yourself asking: Where do I start? What steps do I take? What happens if I fail?

This chapter will guide you through creating a roadmap for your calling. It's not about solving every problem upfront but about taking the next right step. We'll explore the principles of taking risks, staying motivated, and trusting God as you navigate challenges and build momentum.

The Roadmap to Your Calling

Every significant journey begins with a decision to move forward. You might not have the entire map, but you can start by focusing on three essential steps: identifying your next action, staying connected to your motivation, and committing to consistent effort.

THE SLANT METHOD

1. Identify Your Next Action

The first step toward your calling is often the hardest because it requires leaving the safety of the familiar. It's easy to overthink and get stuck in "paralysis by analysis." But clarity doesn't come from standing still because it comes from movement.

Start by asking yourself: What small action can I take today to move closer to my purpose? It doesn't have to be monumental. Whether it's scheduling a meeting, making a phone call, or setting aside time to pray, small actions create momentum.

For example, if your calling involves starting a business, your next action might be researching your target audience or outlining your first product. If it's about strengthening relationships, it could be initiating a meaningful conversation with a loved one. Whatever it is, don't wait for the perfect moment. Start now.

2. Stay Motivated

Pursuing your calling requires endurance, and endurance requires motivation. The key is to identify what drives you. Are you motivated by external rewards, like seeing tangible results? Or do internal factors, like a sense of purpose and alignment with God's will, fuel you more?

Motivation often combines internal drivers, like glorifying God, with external impacts, such as serving others. Recognize and revisit your motivation regularly, especially during tough moments.

Ask yourself: Why does this matter to me? How does this align with who God is calling me to be? The answers will remind you why the hard work is worth it. Dreaming is the easy part when the road is clear. It's only when you hit obstacles that you begin to quit or slow down. That feeling that tries to get you to avoid the hard work is normal. Some call it procrastination. Others call it avoidance. I call it resistance.

In his book, The War of Art, Steven Pressfield sheds light on resistance and how to overcome it. He writes, "The most important thing about art is to work. Nothing else matters except sitting down every day and trying."

Navigating your calling is the hardest part. It requires energy, discipline, and focus. You will want to give up when things don't go your way. But it's in those moments that you must push forward. The hard work of navigating your calling is what separates those who live with purpose from those who let resistance win.

Overcoming Challenges

The journey toward your calling will not be free of obstacles. Whether it's fear, doubt, or unexpected setbacks, challenges are inevitable, but they're also opportunities for growth.

Facing Fear and Doubt

Fear often whispers to you, "What if I fail?" Another voice of doubt asks you, "Are you even capable of this?" These voices can paralyze you, but they don't have to define you. One way to silence fear is by taking risks and trusting God with the outcome. As you step into the unknown, remind yourself that God equips those He calls. Even if you stumble, He uses every experience to shape you.

Staying the Course

Challenges test your commitment. When the road gets tough, it's tempting to give up or take shortcuts. But consistency builds resilience. It's about showing up every day, even when progress feels slow.

To stay the course, surround yourself with accountability. This could be a mentor, a friend, or a community that encourages you and holds you to your commitments. Challenges become more manageable when you're not facing them alone.

In the Bible, the Apostle Paul experienced numerous hardships: imprisonments, beatings, and even being shipwrecked. Before living for Christ, Paul persecuted Christians. When he lived for himself, he navigated minimal opposition. But when he gave his life to the Lord and began to fulfill his calling, he encountered excruciating challenges.

Paul writes in Philippians 3:12, "Not that I have already obtained this or am already perfect, but I press on to make it my own, because Christ Jesus has made me his own." Pressing on must become a natural rhythm for you. No one fulfills their purpose by quitting, wasting time, or complaining. Paul could have given up, abandoned his faith, and returned to persecuting Christians. However, his calling was so great that he was willing to endure the hardships to serve the Lord.

What about you? Are you willing to be misunderstood, betrayed, mocked, endure hurtful comments, or face struggles to fulfill your calling? I encourage you to think about the alternative

A Life Almost Lived

What would it look like for you to give up? How would it affect you, your family, your friends, and others who need you? What about the people who are praying to God for a solution to their problem, and God wants to use you to help solve it? Sadly, they will keep waiting until someone else answers the call.

Years from now, you might sit in regret, wishing you had taken action on the signal. You sit there contemplating where it all went wrong. The feeling of desperation grips your stomach. You wish you could turn back the clock, but you know you can't. You beat yourself up for wasting years because you were afraid or didn't take your calling seriously. You placed others' opinions of you higher than what God says about you. The pain of watching others live out their calling while you avoided yours becomes the deepest regret of your life.

Reflecting on the regret of a life almost lived reminds us of the critical need to stay intentional and focused on our calling. It's not enough to simply feel motivated. We need practical tools to navigate the path forward and overcome the resistance that inevitably arises. This is where frameworks come into play.

Frameworks to Stay on Track

Frameworks provide clarity, structure, and direction, helping you stay on track even when challenges threaten to derail you. One such framework is the SMARTER framework, a powerful tool to ensure that your goals align with your calling and are designed for sustainable success.

In 2018, I attended a conference for high-achievers that

completely changed the way I approached my goals. I had heard of Michael Hyatt before, but I wasn't prepared for how his SMARTER Goals framework would revolutionize my life. During the Your Best Year Ever Live event, Hyatt shared a startling statistic: you are 42% more likely to achieve your goals simply by writing them down. That one fact opened my eyes to the power of intentionality and clarity.

Once I learned this framework, my life transformed in ways I couldn't have imagined. Here's what happened after I started applying SMARTER Goals:

- I published my first book, Pain Formation: Forming Pain into Purpose.
- I achieved my goal of taking several family vacations each year, creating meaningful memories with my loved ones.
- I earned my master's degree in organizational leadership while balancing work and family.
- I trained and signed up for a 30-mile bike race (more on this story later).
- I developed a consistent morning routine that includes Bible study, prayer, and journaling.
- I began regularly publishing content online to share my message.
- I pursued my goals with greater focus, clarity, and intention.

The SMARTER Goals framework gave me a clear path forward, turning my ambitions into actionable plans. It wasn't just about writing goals down. It was about crafting goals that were specific, measurable, and aligned with my purpose.

What Are SMARTER Goals?

Michael Hyatt's SMARTER Goals framework builds on the classic SMART goal system (Specific, Measurable, Achievable, Relevant, and Time-bound) by adding two critical elements: Exciting and Risky. These additional elements ensure your goals are both motivating and challenging, pushing you to grow while staying aligned with your purpose.

- Specific: Your goals must be clear and focused. Ambiguity leads to confusion and inaction. For example, instead of saying, "I want to improve my relationships," write, "I will schedule a weekly one-on-one date night with my spouse."
- Measurable: Goals should have criteria that let you track progress. "I will read 12 books this year" is measurable, while "I want to read more" is not.
- Achievable: While goals should stretch you, they should also be realistic given your current resources and circumstances.
- Relevant: Your goals should align with your values and calling. Ask yourself: Does this goal support the purpose God has placed in my life?
- Time-bound: Set a deadline to create urgency and accountability. Deadlines turn dreams into actionable plans.
- Exciting: Goals should energize and inspire you. They need to connect with your passions or bring joy in the pursuit.
- Risky: Growth happens outside of your comfort zone. A risky goal should push you to rely on God's strength and provision, challenging you to a new level.

Applying SMARTER Goals to Your Life

Let's bring this framework to life with an example:

Goal: Build stronger relationships with my team at work.

Specific: Schedule monthly one-on-one check-ins with each team member.

Measurable: Complete 12 check-ins with each team member by the end of the year.

Achievable: Dedicate one afternoon a month to these meetings.

Relevant: Stronger relationships lead to better team cohesion and reflect my calling as a servant leader.

Time-bound: Begin the first check-in by February 1.

Exciting: Imagine the trust and connection these meetings will build over time.

Risky: Being vulnerable and open in these meetings, even when it's uncomfortable.

The SMARTER Goals framework is about aligning your actions with your identity and calling. By writing down clear, actionable goals and committing to them, you'll not only stay on track but also experience exponential growth in the areas that matter most.

If you're ready to move forward in your calling, start by

writing down one goal using this framework. It's a small step, but it could be the catalyst for the clarity and momentum you've been waiting for.

Writing Down Goals and Building Systems

Writing down your goals is an important step. Each goal serves a purpose: to inspire action and develop life-changing habits. As James Clear states in his book Atomic Habits, "You do not rise to the level of your goals. You fall to the level of your systems."

Think of driving as a metaphor. Goals are the destination you see through the windshield, giving you direction and purpose. Your habits are the engine, wheels, and every working part of the car that moves you forward and ultimately get you to where you want to go.

This connection between goals and systems is vital. While your goals point you in the right direction, it's the daily habits and disciplines you create that provide the fuel and momentum to navigate toward your calling. By combining the clarity of written goals with the consistency of systems, you'll build a foundation for sustainable success.

Craig Groeschel – Clarity Creates Capacity

Craig Groeschel is one of the most influential church leaders in the world. He founded Life.Church, the ministry behind the YouVersion Bible app, and leads a church with dozens of campuses and tens of thousands in attendance each week. But Craig didn't get there by winging it. In fact, early in his leadership, he almost burned out. He had vision, but no roadmap. The church was growing fast, but his pace was unsustainable. He was constantly reacting, trying to do everything himself, and juggling too many roles. Craig admits that the breakthrough didn't come from more hustle, it came from more clarity.

He began writing down his goals. Not vague dreams like "grow the church" or "reach more people." He had specific and measurable outcomes tied to consistent systems. Then came his famous quote: "You don't rise to the level of your goals. You fall to the level of your systems." What changed? Everything.

He created a written structure for preaching, built systems to empower his team, and implemented repeatable rhythms. That structure multiplied him. Clarity scaled his impact. If someone like Craig can get overwhelmed without a plan, so can you. The difference is that he didn't stay stuck. He wrote it down. He built systems. He aligned his actions with his calling.

The vision God gives you is holy. But without a plan, even the holiest vision can die in your notebook or worse, in your head.

Why People Don't Write It Down

Most high-achievers think about their goals constantly, but few actually write them down. Why?

Fear of Commitment
"If I write it down, I'm locked in."
They worry that committing on paper means they can't change course. even if God redirects their path.

Fear of Failure
"What if I don't hit the goal?"
Writing it down makes the dream real and so does the fear of falling short.

Lack of Clarity
"I don't know exactly what I want."
They haven't slowed down long enough to articulate what success looks like.

Belief That It Doesn't Matter
"I've got it all in my head."
But clarity without documentation is fog. It may feel clear today, but without a record, it fades with time and pressure.

A dream not written down is just a wish. A path not planned is just potential wasted.

Writing it down is about permission. It gives you the permission to move forward with intention.

Application: Turning Insights into Action

Now that you've explored the importance of navigating your calling, it's time to put what you've learned into practice. Use these prompts to reflect and take action:

How has resistance stopped you from navigating your calling? Reflect on moments when procrastination, fear, or doubt (resistance) held you back. Write down specific examples and consider what steps you can take to push through when resistance shows up again.

Are you more internally or externally motivated?
Identify the factors that drive you. Is your motivation rooted in internal values like honoring God and fulfilling your purpose, or do external outcomes like helping others or achieving success fuel you? Write a short paragraph about what motivates you most and how you can stay connected to it.

Write down five goals using the SMARTER framework. Take a few minutes to apply the SMARTER framework to five meaningful goals in your life. Ensure your goals are specific, measurable, achievable, relevant, time-bound, exciting, and risky.

Example:
Goal: Strengthen my relationship with my spouse.

Specific: Schedule a weekly date night for the next three months.

Measurable: Track 12 date nights by the end of the quarter.

Achievable: Set aside one evening per week and plan simple, meaningful activities.

Relevant: Reflects my value of prioritizing family relationships.

Time-bound: Start this week, with the first date night scheduled by Friday.

Exciting: Imagine the joy and connection these nights will create.

Risky: Be vulnerable and initiate conversations about deeper topics.

Goals are good. Systems are king.

If goals are like a plane, then systems are the engine. Goals define what you want to achieve, while systems determine how you'll achieve it. You need both to fully step into your calling. Writing your goals on a piece of paper or typing them into a document is just the beginning. The real work starts when you put systems in place to bring those goals to life.

Let me give you an example of a system that helped me reach a goal. In 2022, I signed up for Pedal Hilton Head Island, a 30-mile bike race. Now, I tend to be more ambitious than the average person, especially considering I had never ridden 30 miles on a bike before. I signed up in hopes of a thrilling challenge and I got it.

The next day, I rode my Peloton for 30 minutes and felt accomplished. However, the following day, I didn't want to ride. Why? I couldn't find my bike shorts or my clip-in shoes. As I aimlessly searched my room (purposely wasting time), I eventually found them, but another issue arose because I didn't have a plan. I had no idea how to build up to 30 miles, which, at my pace, would take two hours and forty-five minutes to complete. At that moment, I realized I didn't need another goal. I needed systems. Here's what I did:

Organized my biking shoes, shorts, shirt, water, and Apple Watch the night before each ride.

Created a plan to ride 10 miles for a week, then 15 miles, gradually building up to 30 miles.

Scheduled two 30-mile practice rides (one indoor and one outdoor).

Booked my hotel for the race.

Began a stretching routine.

Pre-decided my diet and snacks for rides of 15 miles or longer.

With these systems in place, I was confident, prepared, and

focused on race day.

Your goal may not be a bike race, but the principle remains the same: systems are critical to success. You can't wish your way to achievement or hope your way to progress. Systems keep you moving forward, maintaining momentum toward your desired outcome. Whether your goal is a deeper relationship with your spouse, a more aligned staff, or a closer walk with God, a solid system will help you get there faster and more effectively.

What are some systems you will create to pursue these goals? Goals require consistent effort to bring them to life.

Write down 2–3 small, daily habits for each of your SMARTER goals.

Example: For the date night goal, your habits might include:

Spending 10 minutes every Monday brainstorming ideas for the week's date.

Setting a recurring reminder to ask your spouse about their availability.

Clarity is the beginning, but strategy is what carries it forward. If you're ready to map out a focused, personalized plan for aligning your team or reimagining your leadership, visit www.JamesMWilson.com. I offer strategic coaching and organizational workshops that bring vision into motion. Your next chapter deserves more than a to-do list. Let's design a blueprint that matches your calling.

CHAPTER 7: TRANSFORM – BECOMING WHO YOU'RE CALLED TO BE

Now that you have completed the first four steps, you've arrived at the final one: Transform. Accomplishing your calling requires becoming a new person. The old version of you cannot meet such high demands. However, as you move toward your aspirations and navigate the terrain, transformation occurs. You become a new person: a different version of yourself. On the other side of discomfort lies a better spouse, parent, Christ-follower, leader, entrepreneur, and friend. But before these changes take place, you'll need a mindset shift.

You must align your mindset with your calling. Do you remember the identity piece we covered in Chapter One? Your mindset needs to connect to a new identity. Why? Because someone living in their calling understands that you never truly "arrive." Yes, you accomplish goals and hit milestones, but if you have breath in your lungs, the work isn't done. You must move from one mountaintop to the next valley to reach the next summit. Why? Because you are a SLANT Leader.

THE SLANT METHOD

Who is a SLANT Leader?

Unbeknownst to you, the framework you've followed isn't random; it's a way of life. These are the steps to clarify your calling:

Signal

Look & Listen

Aspire

Navigate

Transform

S.L.A.N.T.

"Slant" means to diverge from the vertical or horizontal.

The purpose of the chapters was to walk you through a framework filled with principles to stand the test of time. No matter what season of life you are in, the SLANT method is a guide to get you clarity.

A Normal Person: I call them "Normies". Normies drift through life, fail to make plans, avoid self-improvement, and adopt a victim mindset. They leave outcomes to chance and use hope as their only strategy for growth. Their critical to anyone pursuing a better path. They're all talk and no action. They believe things will improve on their own, look for handouts, and make excuses. They blame others for their mistakes, fail to take responsibility, and live day-to-day with their head in the sand, wasting time.

A SLANT Leader: Lives with intention and focus. Understands that life isn't about perfection but progress. They pursue growth in every area of life, take ownership of their mistakes, and fail forward. They have a relentless passion for personal development, keep God and family as their priorities, and strive for wisdom at all costs. They live each day as if it were their last, using their gifts to serve God and lead others.

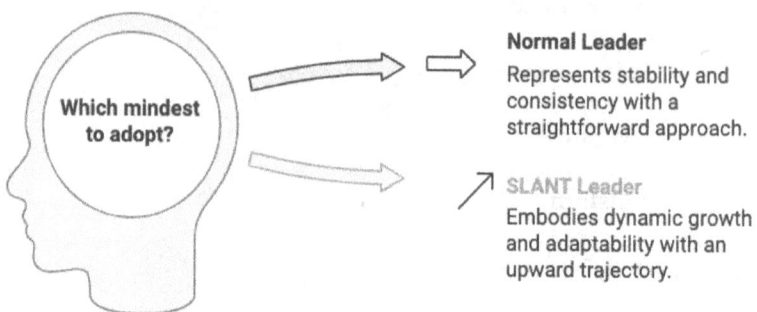

James Clear – From Broken to Becoming

James Clear didn't set out to become a best-selling author or global thought leader. In fact, his story began with trauma. In high school, James was struck in the face by a baseball bat during a freak accident. The injury was devastating as he had broken bones, memory loss, and seizures. His promising athletic career vanished overnight. He spent months in recovery, lost in uncertainty, and unsure of who he even was anymore.

That's when he realized something: he couldn't go back to who he was before, but he could choose who he would become. He started showing up consistently. Small habits. Simple actions. He worked out even when he didn't feel like it. He studied. He journaled. He rewired his life, one behavior at a time. He wasn't trying to "change his life" overnight. He was casting votes for a new identity.

Eventually, he wrote Atomic Habits, a book that's sold millions of copies. But that wasn't the point. The real victory was that he became the kind of man who lived with intention, discipline, and peace.

He writes:

"Every action you take is a vote for the type of person you want to become."

That's the heart of transformation. You don't earn a new identity; you grow into it. One small, faithful step at a time.

Why Identity Change Feels Risky

Most people don't resist growth because they're lazy. They resist it because it feels dangerous.

Fear of Rejection
"Who will I be if I'm no longer that person?"
We worry that the people around us won't accept the transformed version of us, especially if they've benefited from the old one.

Comfort with Dysfunction
"At least I know this version of me."
Even when our habits hurt us, they can feel familiar. And familiar feels safe.

Insecurity About Change
"What if I can't sustain this?"
Transformation feels exciting until we realize it requires consistency, not just emotion.

Identity change isn't just about who you're becoming. It's about being willing to let go of the version of you that's familiar, but no longer faithful. God doesn't just want to improve you. He wants to renew you. That means releasing the old and stepping into who He says you are. Trust the Process

You might be thinking to yourself, "What if I fail?" Let me assure you that you will. We all do. The difference is what you decide to do after the failure. No one is born a SLANT Leader. It's not in your DNA. It's forged in the fire of missed deadlines, shattered confidence, painful pivots, and hard-earned lessons.

You don't become a SLANT Leader by avoiding failure. You become one by learning how to fail forward. You take the path most people avoid; the uncomfortable, inconvenient, often unglamorous path of excellence. Because excellence comes as a cost.

Les Miles once said, "If you want a hard life, do the easy things. If you want an easy life, do the hard things." It's not easy to get up earlier to write that vision. It's not easy to lead when no one's clapping. It's not easy to have the hard conversations, to take the risk, to say no to comfort and yes to purpose. But let me be real with you:

You will never transform doing the easy things. Growth doesn't live in the shallow end of comfort. It lives in the deep waters of discipline. You don't drift into transformation. You decide your way there. One of the hardest battles you'll face won't be with your calendar or your circumstances, it will be with your thinking.

That's why we started with identity and mindset. Because if you don't believe you're capable, if you don't see yourself as someone who is called, if you still wear the name tags of your past such as failure, quitter, not enough, you will sabotage the very thing God is trying to do in your life. You must renew your mind. You must see yourself the way God sees you. You must trust the process even when it's slow. Even when it hurts. Even when you can't see the results yet.

Remember: A seed planted in the ground doesn't look like much... but give it time. So don't resent the process. Respect it. Don't shortcut the struggle. Show up for it. Because you are becoming, and every step you take is proof that God's not done with you yet.

I've seen this happen in real time. When someone stops drifting and steps into alignment, the results can be immediate. One business owner I worked with had a team stuck in confusion and doubt. Team members couldn't decide their weekly sales target. Confidence was low, goals were unclear, and tension was rising. But through just one alignment session, everything shifted. The team gained clarity, restored trust, and left with shared ownership of their mission. After a week, I called the business owner to see how things were going. He exclaimed, "James, you won't believe this, but we just hit our best numbers of the entire year!" He thanked me. This shift did not happen because of a fancy new strategy, but because his team got clear, confident, and committed. That's the power of transformation. Instead of years, they renewed their mindset in hours. It can happen faster than you think!

You Were Made for This

You've come a long way, not just through this chapter, but through a journey of rediscovery. You've paused to evaluate where you've been, dug deep to confront what's been holding you back, and looked forward with fresh clarity about who you're becoming. If you've made it this far, I want to remind you of something important: you're not behind. You're not too late. You're not disqualified. You're becoming and that matters more than you know.

Transformation doesn't happen in a moment of hype. It happens in the quiet decisions. It's forged in early mornings, difficult conversations, unseen sacrifices, and ordinary days when you choose to keep going even when no one is watching. The world celebrates fast results, but God values faithful steps. And while you may not see instant change, don't mistake slowness for failure. Deep roots always grow before visible fruit appears. That's what the SLANT Method has been about from the beginning: alignment. It's a framework to help you move forward with clarity and conviction.

You've seen how easy it is to drift. To settle. To stay in environments that are comfortable but not life-giving. But now you've been given a new path. You know how to recognize the signals, reflect on the past, define your aspirations, chart a path forward, and grow into the leader you were born to be. You are no longer wandering. You are walking with intention. The question is simple: "Will you keep going?"

You can close this book and go back to what's familiar. Or you can move forward into the life God's been calling you into. This path requires faith, grit, and a willingness to grow. Not in theory. But in practice. Every day. One decision at a time.

This isn't the end of your story. It's the beginning of your next chapter. You've got the clarity. You've got the tools. And most importantly, you've got the calling. Show up. Lead well. Love deeply. Think boldly. Live differently. Because this world doesn't need more gurus, it needs more people walking in purpose. You were made for this.

CHAPTER 8: THE LIES THAT KEEP YOU STUCK

Progress Over Perfection

All high achievers have a sickness. We desire growth. We chase solutions. We're addicted to optimization. But here's the shadow side: that pursuit of growth can mutate into an obsession. And when it does, it becomes a silent tormentor. We demand that it happens at our pace, on our timeline, and at our level of expectation. Anything less? Feels like failure. And that, my friend, is a trap.

We start comparing where we are to where we think we should be. We scroll through other people's wins and start resenting our own process. We beat ourselves up for not being farther along, for not being faster, sharper, stronger. And slowly, we begin to forget the beauty of becoming. When perfection is your goal, you'll always feel behind. It's a toxic cycle. Perfection breeds procrastination. You wait, tweak, overthink. You obsess over angles and optics. You get so caught up trying to make it right that you don't move at all.

And then comes burnout. Disappointment. Shame. Guilt.

You miss out on meaningful moments because you're trapped in a never-ending loop of "not yet." Here's the hard truth: The more you obsess over perfection, the more disconnected you become from what matters most. I've been there.

I've had those "golden ideas." You know the ones. The ideas that feel so brilliant they could change the world. The ones you talk about nonstop. The ones you color-code in notebooks, pitch to friends, dream about in the shower. You analyze them. Marinate on them. Share them in mastermind groups. But you don't move.

You feel productive because your brain is working. But your hands aren't doing anything. And deep down, you know it: your obsession with getting it just right is keeping you stuck. It's not execution. It's performance anxiety in disguise. You're afraid to start because you don't want to fail. You're afraid to move because what if it's not perfect?

Waiting for perfection doesn't lead to excellence; it leads to delay, discouragement, and disobedience. Let me say this as clearly as I can: Waiting on perfection is imperfection. God never asked you to be perfect. He asked you to be faithful. That means showing up. Even when it's messy. Even when you're unsure. Even when you only have 70% clarity.

Because transformation is a process. It's a lifelong progression. You don't become who you're called to be overnight. You become one decision, one disciplined step at a time. That's why progress must become your ally. Progress doesn't mean doing it all today. It means doing something. Progress doesn't mean being the best. It means being better. Progress means you're becoming the kind of person who keeps going even when it's hard. And here's the good news: God doesn't grade you on perfection. He watches how you respond in the process.

Remember Philippians 1:6?

"He who began a good work in you will bring it to completion at the day of Jesus Christ." (ESV)

God didn't start something in you just to leave you halfway. But you've got to keep moving. Don't wait for permission. Don't wait for perfect. Start. Even if it's ugly. Even if it's small. Even if no one claps. Because every step of progress is a vote for the person you're becoming.

Imposter Syndrome Is a Lie

Let's deal with one last lie before we close: Imposter Syndrome.

Have you ever said…

"I'm an imposter."

"I can't do this."

"I'm not good enough."

"I'm going to mess this up."

"I don't have what it takes."

"People will see right through me."

"Someone else is better equipped for this than me."

Those aren't just thoughts. They're lies cleverly packaged to sound like humility. But they're rooted in fear, not truth. And if you let them stay, they'll sabotage your progress and paralyze your purpose. Here's what most people don't realize:

Imposter Syndrome isn't a medical diagnosis. It's a scarcity mindset. It is fear dressed up as logic. It's the enemy planting doubt in your identity so you'll shrink back from the assignment God gave you.

And it sounds convincing. It tells you that because you've made mistakes in the past, you're disqualified. It whispers that you're too young, too old, too inexperienced, too late. It makes you second-guess what God already confirmed. You're not an imposter. You're in process. Every leader you admire felt this way at some point. Moses did. Gideon did. Jeremiah did. Even Paul had moments where he questioned whether he was worthy of his calling.

God has a long track record of using people who felt underqualified:

Moses stuttered, but God made him a voice for the nation.

Peter denied Jesus three times, but God made him the rock of the church.

Paul persecuted believers, but God used him to write most of the New Testament.

What do they all have in common? They weren't perfect. They were obedient. That's the invitation: not to be flawless, but to be faithful. You don't have to be fully formed to be fully called. You don't need every credential before you take your first step. You just need to say "yes" to God and trust Him with the details. Because at the end of the day, God doesn't call the qualified, He qualifies the called.

If He put the desire in your heart...
If He opened the door...

If He's stirring something inside of you right now…

Then you belong in the room. You're not pretending. You're not faking it. You're becoming.

Transformation on an Airplane

A few years ago, I met a woman on a flight back to Atlanta, GA. She was reading *Can't Hurt Me* by David Goggins. As a fellow high achiever, I told her I loved that book, and we struck up a conversation. What began as small talk about life and work quickly shifted into something deeper.

She told me she was an elementary school teacher. She liked her job, but something in her tone revealed she felt unfulfilled. As we talked, I began asking her questions guided by the SLANT framework. Finally, she admitted, "I've always wanted to go into real estate. My dad is very successful and has even offered to help me, but... I just can't do it." In that moment, it became clear: she wasn't just stuck, she was scared. Fear had taken hold, and her disbelief was shaping her actions. "What are you afraid of?" I asked. "What if it doesn't work?" she whispered. "Alex," I replied, "you seem like the type of person who gets things done no matter what. So how much longer are you going to waste time feeling stuck?"

We talked the entire flight. When we landed, we exchanged goodbyes and went our separate ways. Months later, my inbox lit up with a Facebook message. It was Alex. She told me she had left teaching and stepped into real estate. But that wasn't all. She was already ranked among the top 50 REMAX agents in her state.

God had orchestrated that meeting. The calling was already in her. It just needed to be unlocked. Fear had held her back, but a few questions shifted everything. Today, she's not only successful, she's fulfilled. She's living in her calling and making a real impact. And here's the truth: Alex isn't unique. She's just like you. The only difference was a choice. She chose to stop letting fear decide her future. Now the question is… will you?

CHAPTER 9: DON'T JUST CLARIFY—COMMIT

Take a moment to breathe and look back on the path you've just traveled. Over these pages you have moved from drifting to deciding, from simply wondering about your place to actively walking toward it. You came because something in your spirit insisted there had to be more peace, more purpose, more alignment between the life you lead, and the one God designed for you. That intuition was correct, and now the landscape in front of you looks different than it did when you began.

With that new perspective comes a choice. One direction returns you to the familiar rhythms that once felt safe but quietly kept you stuck. The other leads forward into obedience and transformation, a route that promises depth but refuses the comfort of cruise control. Many people hesitate at this point because clarity always carries responsibility. Once you see the truth, you can't pretend you haven't. Questions start to surface: Do I really have the time? What if I stumble again? Was that nudge from God, or just wishful thinking? Most of these questions are simply fear disguised as logic, urging you back to the status quo. The alternative is to answer fear with a decision.

Throughout this book you have practiced hearing the Signal that something was off, pausing to Listen and Learn from your story, daring to Aspire to a vision that reflects your values, and plotting how to Navigate the realities of calling in everyday life. You have discovered that transformation is not a one-time adrenaline rush but a holy, ongoing process powered by daily faithfulness. These lessons have already begun reshaping how you see yourself, your work, and the people entrusted to your influence.

Now the work shifts from discovery to consistency. Transformation will live or die in small, quiet choices such as setting the alarm, guarding your calendar, voicing the hard truth, surrendering an outcome in prayer, celebrating a team member's win, or simply showing up when no spotlight is on you. Those choices compound into character, and character becomes the platform God uses to multiply your impact. If at any point the road feels hazy, return to the questions and frameworks you've learned here. Clarity is rarely found in a single lightning bolt; it grows each time you realign your thoughts, words, and habits with the identity God has already spoken over you.

You don't drift into your calling; you decide and keep deciding, one faithful step at a time. May the clarity you've gained propel you into a life marked by purpose, peace, and the unmistakable presence of God in everything you build.

A Quick Story Before You Go...

Let me tell you about a woman I recently coached. She owns a small retail shop and felt deeply called to help people heal naturally, but she was stuck. Passionate? Absolutely. But without a clear vision, she was just going through the motions. I had an opportunity to coach her to draw out what was already in her heart.

By the end of our time, she had written out a powerful vision statement for her business. It wasn't just about business success, it was about becoming one of the top herbal medicine companies in the country, building a team so she could focus on being a registered herbalist, and using her work to glorify God. Later, she posted her experience on social media:

"God has put some really cool people in my life—especially those who won't leave my shop until I write out my vision and let them tweak it. Words are powerful. All I want to do is make medicine and glorify God. Here's to making serious changes and keeping my eye on the vision ahead. He will indeed lead the way."

She didn't just get clarity. She got conviction. She got alignment. That's what happens when you finally put language to the thing God's been whispering to your soul for years. You stop drifting and start becoming. You realize you were never crazy; you were just called.

That's the power of walking in clarity. It changes you and everyone around you. That's why I believe so deeply in this work. Because when one person gets aligned, it creates a ripple effect. In their marriage. In their team. In their church. In their legacy. And now… that ripple starts with you.

From Calling to Commission

Jesus didn't say, "Come follow me, and I'll give you clarity." He said, "Come follow me, and I'll make you fishers of men." Clarity isn't the final step because it's what prepares you for commission. The question isn't "Do you have a calling?" You do. The question is, "Will you walk in it?" You've already received what you need to begin. Take the next step. If you're not sure what that next step looks like, I want to personally help.

Let's Keep Going—Together

If you're ready to stop drifting and start moving with purpose, I invite you to join me in one of these ways:

Private Executive Coaching

For high-achieving professionals or purpose-driven entrepreneurs who want 1:1 support to clarify their next move and take bold action.

Team Alignment Consulting

If you lead a team that's misaligned, I'll help you eliminate confusion and build a culture of clarity, ownership, and performance.

Start your journey at: www.JamesMWilson.com

Don't just clarify your calling.
Commit to it.

Because your calling isn't a theory. It's a commission. And your next chapter is waiting to be written by you.

Now go live it.

ABOUT THE AUTHOR

James Wilson is the Founder of Slant Leadership Group, Executive Pastor at First Baptist Church Powder Springs, and Leadership Development Partner at TCI Solutions. Creator of the SLANT Method, he equips leaders to move from confusion to conviction, aligning their lives with purpose and leading with confidence. He lives in Metro Atlanta, Georgia, with his family.

ACKNOWLEDGMENTS

First and foremost, I thank God for His love, mercy, and patience with me. This book is not the product of human effort alone, but of grace, conviction, and divine alignment. Every word is a testimony to His faithfulness.

To my wife, Alison. Thank you for your unwavering love, patience, and belief in me. Your support gave me the space to write, the encouragement to finish, and the inspiration to keep going. I wouldn't be the man I am without you.

To Eli, Ellie, and Ethan. You are my "why." Every page of this book was written with you in mind. I want you to know that purpose matters more than performance, and that clarity comes when you walk closely with the Lord.

This book was not created with a team behind me. It was written in the margins of busy days, during quiet nights, and in the sacred tension between calling and responsibility. It is for the Lord and for my family, and I wouldn't have it any other way.

ENDNOTES

Chapter 2 – Calling vs. Purpose

1. Dharius Daniels, Your Purpose Is Calling: Your Difference Is Your Destiny (Zondervan, 2019).
2. Craig Groeschel, Divine Direction: 7 Decisions That Will Change Your Life (Zondervan, 2017).

Chapter 5 – Aspire

1. George T. Doran, "There's a S.M.A.R.T. Way to Write Management's Goals and Objectives," Management Review (1981).
2. Michael Hyatt, Your Best Year Ever: A 5-Step Plan for Achieving Your Most Important Goals (Baker Books, 2018).
3. Howard Schultz, Onward: How Starbucks Fought for Its Life without Losing Its Soul (Rodale Books, 2011).
4. Steven Pressfield, The War of Art: Break Through the Blocks and Win Your Inner Creative Battles (Black Irish Entertainment LLC, 2002).

Chapter 6 – Navigate

1. Stephen R. Covey, The 7 Habits of Highly Effective People (Simon & Schuster, 1989).

www.ingramcontent.com/pod-product-compliance
Lightning Source LLC
Chambersburg PA
CBHW071121160426
43196CB00013B/2655